In the Frail

by
erinn
kathryn

know
your
local

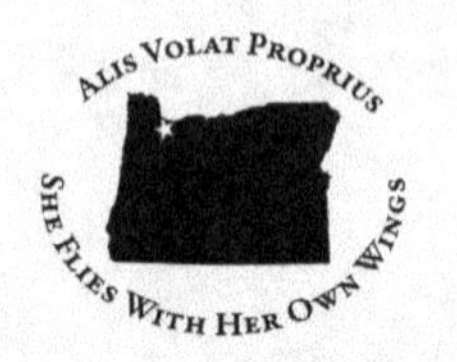

Congratulations! A Buckman production is in your hands! We're an unorthodox operation that continues the daredevil tradition of literature, printing new sparks that ignite imagination. Proudly independent, Buckman's defiant attitude aims to inspire and increase readership in greater society.

read this book wherever books can be read

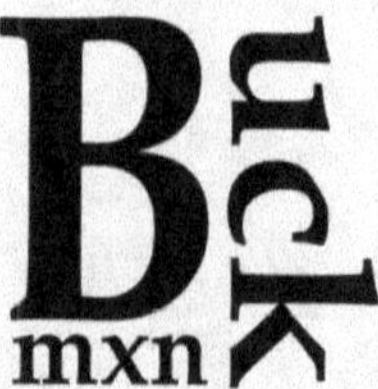

Buckman operates from our home in the upper left of Turtle Island at the confluence of the Whilamut and Wimahl rivers, among the waters and lands of the Cayuse, Clackamas, Multnomah, St'pulmsh (Cowlitz) Umatilla, Walla Walla, and Watlala peoples.

In the Frail

constructed poems

erinn kathryn

Table of Contents

Foreword

Essence

There are an estimated 170,000 words in use in the English language today—and that's not even to mention the many obsoletes—meaning: for the modern language artist, the material is vast, even overwhelming. So one can understand the impulse to winnow the palette; to establish a container from which to summon and craft within. A way of not taming, but perhaps culling the imagination, guiding the composition by providing already arranged sequences of words that offer themselves up for reception, reinterpretation, renewal. Language as the ever-malleable, truly inexhaustible form.

Multiple poetic methods of practicing this renewal have evolved in the last century, including erasure and blackout poetry, which live on the very same page as the original text but take their shape from blacking out lines and phrases to reveal select lines. Erasure is a similar practice of removal/reveal.

The cut-up style of writing that uses words sliced and lifted from an existing text is slightly different in that a new page is required. The language is extracted and rearranged in a fresh setting, from scratch. This linguistic excavation is a Dadaist technique popularized by William Burroughs in the 1950s and 60s; but one that has always existed in an informal sense.[1]

The utensil, in this case, is an exacto knife, and the palette is *Persons and Places* by the prolific 19th and 20th century philosopher, writer, and scholar George Santayana. The book is an account of his own pastiche, the people and landmarks and experiences that influenced his construction of self and his ways of writing, speaking, and theorizing about the self. A poet himself, Santayana was devout in his practice and study of imagination, critical realism, and, as he called them, "the realms of being," so Santayana is a natural repository for the sort of vocabulary poets would want to access. This volume, one of the last books he would publish while alive, acts as the

---

[1] What is each of our own personal languages than a pastiche synthesis of all the other previous arrangements of words we have heard and read and been given, swirled around and repurposed and flowing from our mouths and pens and fast-tapping fingerpads.

prism from which new poems, collected here, are sought out and sculpted, speaking into their new context decades later.

Matter

The cut-up itself is a continuum. A transformative act of threshing one creation into a new likeness. Material that was produced by another artist gets physically rearranged by the current body. It's a simultaneously tactile, ocular, and verbal art. The cut-up acts as a temporal tether, reanimating and repurposing its past, thereby placing the work firmly into existential conversation with the canon. A palimpsest where fused hybrid forms speak cyclically with their antecedents and their audience.

This series transpired in and because of the time it originated from; a project contained in what we have coined "the pandemic years," though we are very much still in them. What we mostly refer to is the slippery months of highest isolation, when our realms of being abruptly condensed, simplified, distilled, reckoning. In the year 2020, communing with this old linen-covered book, and becoming a comb, dredging its pages for some aged meaning to mess with, represent (re-present), even learn from. A deep dialogue when that kind of encounter was rare.

We all became, in a way, ontologically inclined in that time. Without the hours and days and weeks filled, overflowing as they used to be, this was a phase in which we actually tuned in to the condition of the spirit. Singular and collective.[2]

So this was a natural setting to undertake a cross-century collaboration, to become concerned with the spirit, the existence, the channel; what words resound into this lifetime, a next iteration of the text.

Truth

Originally published in 1944, *Persons and Places* was built from language that was in fashion eight decades ago. So, the compositional play at work here echoes postmodernism insomuch as it creates a refraction, mirroring multiple perspectives and compiling them into a piece that may speak with a higher degree of clarity to the complexity of our being.

---

[2] Santayana himself underwent a formative stretch of isolation when he was living in Rome and could not travel or have visitors for years during and after the war.

In a philosophical sense, Santayana resolutely assumed "an aesthetic view of the mind."[3] All styles of erasure fit within this concept in that they represent a form of thinking on the page. In this style, a poet does not sit down to write *about* something but functions more like a sculptor—surveying the source, taking stock of the raw material, and preemptively searching out a separate, latent form which is present, though not yet visible; which will emerge through a series of choices and handmade alterations.

Santayana was concerned with perception and with beauty, one as the threshold into another: "[beauty] exists in perception, and cannot exist otherwise."[4]

The artist's tool here, aside from the handheld ones, is indeed perception; a state of receiving and seeking at once to pluck the words that resonate and preserve them, carry them over into a brand-new poem.

Spirit

"As Santayana argued at length in *Interpretations of Poetry and Religion,* the sphere of the spirit encompassed poetry as well as religion, for the two were different expressions of the same thing."[5]

The poet, critic, and practioner of erasure, Mary Ruefle, in her succinct dictum, *On Imagination*, explains:

> The evolution of our languages—the different languages of the human species—was a great act of imagination that continued enacting itself over a very long period of time and is still enacting itself. At some point in this continuum, when one spoke or wrote the word "tree," the one listening or reading (which is a form of listening) had to see the image of a tree in their mind. Anything involving an image in the head is an act of imagination. We think in both images and words, and since words are imaginary enactments (the word "tree" is not a tree,) thinking and imagining are one.[6]

This illuminates how the mind depends on the inseparability of image and word.

---

[3] Santayana, George. *Realms of Being.* C. Scribner's Sons, 1942.
[4] Santayana, George. *The Sense of Beauty.* Dover Publications, 1955.
[5] McClay, Wilfred. "Remembering Santayana." *The Wilson Quarterly.* vol. 25, no. 3. (Summer 2001).
[6] Ruefle, Mary. *On Imagination.* Sarabande Books, 2017.

With our reliance on language as a species, we have evolved into a naturally hybrid mode of cognition, enabled by imagination.

Imagination's innate presence within our human brains is precisely what allows literature or poetry to transpire, to transmit. A form like the one in this book—in which visual meets textual, employs the practices of an artist but uses the material of a writer—is the embodiment of this type of multi-genre imagining. This volume demonstrates several consciousnesses entwined beyond clear delineations: the poet's own mind, that of the original author, and also now yours, the reader/receiver.

"Santayana reserved his deepest reverence for the products of the imagination."[7] And perhaps that imagination does well with some parameters, with a practice that's tactile and transcendental at once.

---

[7] McClay, Wilfred. "Remembering Santayana." *The Wilson Quarterly.* vol. 25, no. 3. (Summer 2001).

Artist's Note

These works limn the threshold between the written word (poetry) and the art object (visual art), built from the cuttings of one text: *Persons and Places* by George Santayana, which I picked up for a quarter on a "last chance" sale shelf of retired books outside my graduate school's library in 2004.

This selection of pieces comes from my pandemic-era series, titled *In the Frail*, which is still ongoing; just as the subjects it attends to—grief, loneliness, and the pervasive sense of unknowing, political devolution, the warming planet, and frequency of wildfires—are too.

The act of constructing poems from existing text is a longstanding practice of mine, which I return to in difficult emotional times, times of transition, or creative stagnation; all of which were/are elevated by the global pandemic, lockdown, climate crisis, racial injustice, and loss of life. Reconfiguring existing text offers a palette and parameters distinct from sitting down to the blank page; the words and phrases that call out to me reveal insights about my psyche, emotions, and subconscious. This process coincides with my overarching use of found material and allows me to achieve a flow state not unlike that of my visual art practice.

I turned to this exercise to feel like I was still making, and to flesh out and record the world we were (are) enduring. Like diary entries, they catalogue experiential milestones large and small. They wrestle with notions of inside vs. outside, productivity, captivity, creativity, and "otherness." They are an archive of the anxiety, unsettledness, and prostration borne of idle time in a world "on pause" amidst the late Trump administration, Covid-19, fear/loss/death/isolation, Black Lives Matter protests, and climate-crisis events. But these cantos also offer slivers of hope, belief in resiliency, reminders that progress is not linear, and avowal that revolution can begin with a whisper.

I
unknowns

I

in that year,
a year or two
the first two

I feared the world,

on those long afternoons

I mastered

sitting there
and going to bed again.

one foot

formed habits

stone setting into
ground

my hands gathered dust

and I wept,

near-sighted

dull

inside,

we were

translating the tragedy

in real time";

the great landlord

imposed
isolation

the green paradise

was off limits,

the oval suspended our circle

narrowed

as we abandoned

human life humanly.

3

the omens:

dying animals

thaw, and flood
                flood
the coming and going of people,
whose freedom
house and land was
taken
poverty added,
neighboring occupation,
of longstanding colonial culture,

ntensified the general instability of everything.

Self-Portrait as Landscape (for Ocean)
04.05.2022

My particular
meat
body
was half dust
heavy
yellow,
deep
my loss established me
my windows, once glass,
clear,
lighted
lace
lace curtained, now

drooping
crimson
wallpaper
turned
to dingy red leaves
none
patina; my
rooms left vacant
sand—blown
and insecure
the door.

I right myself by
two masts:
before,
the vast and blowing the
luxurious nest of sensitive safety
glowing
touching
dreaming
held,

the now of freedom and
of
mossy stone and granite strong
and fuck it all
all
to reinforce this
house
brick by
brick by
brick by
brick;
better
than to be
deserted.

solitude,
solitude,
solitude.
secluded
lost in seclusion,
alone at home,

in home waters
falling in
staying in
drowning in
in
luxurious,
great lace flounces
she is comfy but
inwardly
alone,
shapeless
sleepless
lit
she serenades the walls
except still
longs to
let go go out
expatriate
wander off, into some decent crowd,
saturated with affectations.
out stretch two arms, embrace
touch, hold tight
longer
re-enact the hug
remain indefinitely desperately
held
weary of this everlasting

freeze:
a vacant year a
harmony in grays

Ruth
11.04.2020

her aged body
withered
against all
will and might
but still her soul
her spirit
full
still
still donned her usual
white lace
with scalloped edges, eighty seven
she knew the stakes
she
much understood
and couldn't
bear it; America
in her white and blue and red silk
cloak of freedom
liberty
has slipped
into a melancholia
limping
hauling
sallow
the silks unravelling
rotting
I cannot save us any more
she whispered
and closed her eyes,
now
take it down and
tell the world.
America:
"Wait till you come to."

I felt
I
was obsolete except for
some ash gray dust
mere remanants to sweep
from a vacant room
once my own
vivid working place
my ideas
they run down my legs and sink
below hard ground
rot
there
in the darkest black
creative hole
half-closed
pandemic - shaped
my idle thoughts
they have no bodies, no
weight / wait;
I breathe into
my own hands, uneasy,
cover both eyes,
and pull back
to see
my elements
almost timid, and dull
and all
the discipline contradicts
my disillusioned
isolated
self.
This prolonged
uncertainty
unyielding, bears
artistic
poverty,
subdued
resignation,
a block
This is not a residency.

II
evidences

The Dark Night
12.21.2020

There is a sort of indifference to time
in the dark night —
the glare and the cold
that run down
surrounding hilltops
dissipates
that we might ride on
but not steadily,
but not easily.

We have

detached
car from train
impermanence from pretending permanence.
Now we're drifting
motorless
counting the passed
over
300,000
grief
quickens
the body
organs
tighten
the air,
resigned
circles
our innumerable loss blot
blot
blots
out the light
we carry
this grave, silent,
solemn
so that each is known
this heavy burden —
we eat at its table,
sleep in its bed.

This is our house,
to live in

until

17

The man who gave the
           group   mind
           a name
           the motive;

ous, budding powers
   beholden to the system
              to secure

  their prosperous, ambitious, enterprising race
            carpeted in scandal
            and long habitual
              idiocies.
      doing his old trick,
        mock   the facts , friends
       at the top,
no matter how many individuals
            suffer
              in perishing.

     this is patriarchal
            occupation

O, particular spring,
unsettled arc of passing
time
some
tightly curling
song
looped
comfortless;

What was I, what were my ?

These rosy sunsets often take
the place of hiding —
the winter's stanza,
a dull routine.

From the windows
I pretend we
are outsiders
again and
practice dressing
running through the house,
then open over the grass
. . .
but
there is
only one angle,
inside

my sentiment satirized
the life of the place,
for we are still kissing
each other
through a mask.

No:
We the people
will not be
the hangman
in
the primitive man's
politics of the hour,
propaganda that intoxicates,
and
needless prejudice
bulging out under it.

No:
no to
the motives
the lying and
unrelenting fatalism
no to praying
at the altar of
perpetual progress and prosperity;
the "bird-witted" clown
dæmonic
man
must
go
down.
We the people
have been
victimized enough;
No.

PHASE III
02.11.2022

III

and one day
from summer
that same year

even, before
we remembered the air
and aspiration fully, before
we got to the last new

exhale   our faces

free, they called us in,
in
the middle of   rejoice —
our impassioned
pillow fights, suspended
at once reduced to a dream, or some
trick of memory,
our
well - earnled
rowdiness
stuck
suffocated
diced and served
a morsel
to hold
sullenly

back

inside

longer

back

to armchair day dreams staring
listlessly at some   novel
expecting   visits
wanting   them

so

this
is season three

25

Settle The Sea
01.2019

heavy, materialistic,
earth bandits

growing rich; people
seduced and distracted

the grand attractions
scattered the
ground, modified
geology

the

material

material

material

running

dark blue

pale blue

curling brown

dry and brittle

sandy heap

concrete reef

strewn with rubbish

and sewage
tides.

the future
an automatism

1/2019

Prophecy
09.13.2020

could be any hour, still
the sun
was a dim
red and sunken in front as to seem
it was not here
at all

again:

yellow tinted horizons dissolved
into paled fire cloud stretches,
that
veil
utterly
the atmosphere
altogether,
dead leaves that scratch on
sealed front door s
articulated prophesy :
warmest
driest
burning
burned

again.

III
conditions

You
01.18.2024

the tone of
water and blood
in the ears
had washed out
days: I mean
it was a day or two before
she
felt the blow.
you, you
and you
who had occupied
long nights
(as I never did)
spared
only a
yellow
of little
which points–
sharp
inverted icicles
some slivers
of bad climate, thin
layers of old chalk
scraped her hand,
pinched her throat, cold and
cracked
and
crawling, a-long
in spite of everything
in the silence.
in the silence
gray footsteps
paced
boots pounded the same circles over
hours,

walking
"sponging" sand blue-water
under
her thirst
how comfortless

how comfortless
but the louder
the

boom,
she let out
and she squished her battered large wings through
oval opening and cried
—for fear of fainting.
for fear
of doing nothing.
no soldier,
no soldier
no soldier

IT ALL WAS ONE WOOF
11.04.2020

It all was one woof;

NINETY DAYS
08.03.2020

Sunday morning in
had taken shape —
ninety days
the two of us,
sleepy,
empty,
spent.

The melancholy
lingered,
anxiety
hollowed out
every room initially.

The walls possess heavy
things that now preoccupy us;
ghosts
those feelings,
the isolation,
our situational fatigue;
our minds and bodies vacant
vessels
empty lots
adorned in ill-kept clothes
worn
like
old notions of reality
finally fading away.

Untitled
06.03.2020

I was
born
with
privilege,
my white body was not made
a weapon
it was never a threat
to officers
in uniform.
But I am not deaf
or blind
I feel the rage
and the drowning in sorrow
sorrow
sorrow

from
secret slavery
intolerance
and blindness
and the memory
of prejudices
painted white,
washed out.
So many young men put to death
died too soon
too soon,
the crowd of witnesses
cannot
recall all the people's names.
The injustice runs deeper.
It must be destroyed.
I believe in change
I ally in revolution
I will march my body out to
transform this wretched system into another —

black lives matter
black lives matter
black lives matter.

Birthday Song
02.20.2024

I didn't know a word
for the young—
I forgot it,
because in the morning,
my face and hands,
their
skins hung heavy down   sallow
now a paper color
a further
thin
transparency
instead of oblong these
ten fingers
performed claws, caught and
pointed stiff,
for instance,
resembling
animal   already
with a narrow chest my
two bags dropped
swinging
slops
the space between them
altogether
they've begun to flag,   and
some odd water in
front of my two
ovals knots the paunch
like an acorn, until I
hit the bath to simmer like
some wallowing hippopotamus
onto the structural:
one shoulder shrank more
than other all round,
affecting immense slanting
a camelback condition for
my feminine figure,
many days a
bye
holding my head
is like
torture
to the neck the forehead
the lips,
the corner the eye
become too heavy for
fortyfour years on me—
all mutations respected an
incongruous wreckage but
they're mine .
praise me
out—

She needed to be carried away, to be
put to bed
to be
out of sight. Her
holy orifice
had aired,
air,
thick
dangling
viscous, it
clung to the nave
to the bowl
" half-sick "
the man said, and
turning into madness.
neglect
of her appearance
only brought it out more clearly.

poor girl.

They think they
know
what parts. They
force
Everything

her cool aisles,
the shell,
the seed
could be saved
must coöperate
man said.
dark red
blot
of ink
pale
of pearls
places
the girl
on deck again, worsted
wanting
for sanctuary.

Self-Portrait In Situ
05.13.2021

So you went
there
all
sugar blown
and held together mechanically
leaning on artificial objects
in some narrow hallway called
healing.
I was obliged to carry you

up
down, when
then,
in the first strata
in which
in the slightest mist

you'd drown.
In the lowness
in the whirl
you left the bathtub the
comfort of water

dazed
wasted
ramshackle
blue,
several shades
blue —
belonging not to
the age
just blank
without mother
still

part of it was your
unruffled perfection
and heavy
despair
beneath the surface,
but always
the loss of
any
forever
while the others
pick their way through:

America,
as a young girl she
would
have posed
firm and distinctive
generous
sensual
kind
nobly guarding every living creature
on earth.

But he
man
without a conscience
immediately
imposed
himself,
disabled her jaw and tongue
dismantled her ribs and sinews
built
phallic towers
of fictitious ascendency over others

She,
unsinkable America
a woman of spirit and will
escaped from it all
retreated to
the valley beneath her windows,
over Sacred land
to a long sea
there
gathered us all in
to forge a revolution

IV
listening

I
make
the voyage
out
immediate for
the
backyard,
for any gray-green
any slender sunlit stretch
a grassy expanse glimpsed
from
another backyard

I close one
eye
squint through a round hole
in the fence
savor some small illusions
that I
am
nearer to mother earth; this
simple summer ceremony
my quarantine pilgrimage

the American man
an instructive guide;

gentlemen,
white
orange
gentleman —

" Warren up".

for the coming week
lose the stupid hat
the foolish flag
the insidious rhetoric
the indulgent self - praise

Behave civilly,
feign dignity,
cry desperately with shame
for undermining truth

Do something.

wear a mask
start
washing those tiny, slovenly hands
confess your crimes and moral evils
practice prudence
(shut your mouth)
quit measuring
your prick
dip
those shriveled
official balls
in the icy river
of some melting glacier

for the sake of
a more urgent need
like the poor,
working classes,
the children
prejudice
injustice
financial crisis
warming climate

for the democracy,
for Goddess's sake.

For once
abandon superior airs
toxic attitudes
ignorance of self
and finally
idiocy.

yours,

women

we should walk
with
the small
breeze.
partake of the hot
night into a dark street
drag heavy cheeks
vital bones
flimsy bodies
stout, placid, like great gilded
sculptures in some old
palazzo
out
to walk,
laugh
at the first loud foot-fall for now
hold hands, sigh
find rest from our weeping;
flood
and
fire
and war
and
resources,
and
bloodstains ;
things close
of the face, for now
accompany me wholly
in the green
opposite:
behold the half round moon
arches,
painting a great
sky
the magnificent clearness
deep
and blue
be at bottom
each a small bowl
save
the dew:
drying
thirsty
mouths went perfectly
we too are made of water.

Phase II
01.31.2022

I I

who pronounced it ?' the
opening because

feeling a little dazed,

having dragged myself down

from

the attic,

that attic

slovenly,

limp,

hair escaping

I got up, leaving out

again,

and the crusts fell off .

remember ?

in opening

how the world

it glittered and it gummered,

in the foreglow and afterglow

and we sang,

and we lived

gloriously,

during?

Here
    in the vortex of a
life in
the surrender
feeling the
tang of hardship,
unrecoverable solitude,
                and
emotional poverty,
and silence;
enthroned.

        As
it got into difficulties,
and the things
small
had proved
devastating,
more than ever,
this
especially
added to distance.

The communal spirit
    restless behind its iron bars,
wishing
            "hurry up."

At bottom there was
    was only a listening;
poetry,
sunset,
dreaming awake.
a piece of paper.

In the
frail
the universe
always leaves some room
to,
at the right hour,
be reborn
and build anew.

Acknowledgments

First and foremost I want to thank Emmi, Ellen, Rich, and Kris at Buckman for helping me realize this project, which I never envisioned moving beyond my own pandemic diary. Thank you also to Alyson Bowen and Borderline Press for ongoing collaboration and support of my desire to always take it one step further. To the Regional Arts & Culture Council for supporting the exhibition of original works. To Drew, Pam, John, and Ara for invaluable feedback and problem solving, and general co-nerdiness in all things art. Last, but definitely not least, to Ryan for being my co-pilot through this world, and for seeing me for all that I can be.

About the Artist

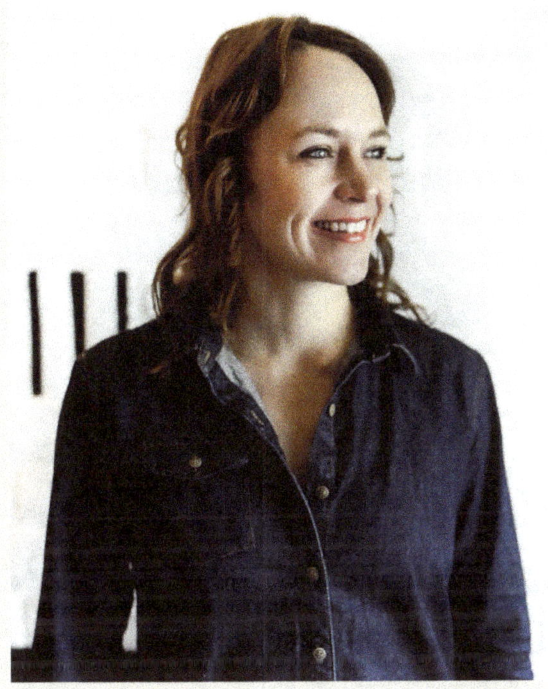

© Roxy Allen

Erinn Kathryn (she/her) is an interdisciplinary artist working in sculpture, mixed media, painting, and installation. She finds, collects, hordes, and augments found materials of all kinds, ranging from mass-produced goods like postcards and blister packs, to natural materials like bones, moss, and lichen to literal street-side garbage and mowed-over children's toys. By re-contextualizing existing objects, Erinn reframes long-held perspectives and examines intersections between the "natural" and "constructed" within which we exist.

In the Frail is Erinn's first published poetry series.